Bảo Anh Lạc Bookshelf 61

THE RITUAL OFFERING FOOD TO HUNGRY GHOSTS

Composed
by

Bhikṣuṇī TN Giới Hương

Hong Duc Publishing

HUONG SEN BUDDHIST TEMPLE
19865 Seaton Avenue
Perris, CA 92570, USA
Tel: 951-657-7272, Cell: 951-616-8620
Email: huongsentemple@gmail.com
thichnugioihuong@yahoo.com
https://www.facebook.com/Huong.Sen.Riverside
Web: www.huongsentemple.com

ISBN: 978-1-0880-9813-4

THE FIRST WORDS

Every day Nuns and Buddhists at Hương Sen Buddhist Temple, California, USA, have practiced and recited following the Vietnamese scripture, "Nghi Lễ Hàng Ngày – 50 Kinh Tụng và các Lễ Vía trong Năm" (Daily Chanting – Fifty Discourses and Annual Festivals) of the Pureland Sect, which was composed in 2021 by Bhikkhunī Thích Nữ Giới Hương. It is based on the original ritual of her late Master, the Venerable Elder Hải Triều Âm at Liên Hoa Temple and Dược Sư Temple.[1]

Since many Vietnamese-Americans, Hispanic, native Americans, and English speakers have come to Huong Sen Temple in search of practice and ritual, Bhikkhunī Giới Hương composed an English version of **DAILY MONASTIC CHANTING**. It encompasses 16 popular rituals to serve the spiritual needs of any Buddhist sect, including the Pure Land and Meditation Traditions as below:

1. Practice Meditation
2. The Ceremony for Peace
3. The Rice Offering to Buddhas
4. The Lunch Offering at the Dining Hall
5. The Ritual Offering Food To Hungry Ghosts
6. The Pureland Course of Amitabha Sutra
7. The Medicine Buddha Sutra
8. The New Year Ceremony

1 Please read: http://www.huongsentemple.com/index.php/vn/phat-phap/kinh-ta-ng-ca-a-cha-a-hs/6256-nghi-le-hang-ngay-20.

9. The Great Parinirvana Ceremony
10. The Buddha's Birthday Ceremony
11. The Ullambana Festival (Parents' Day)
12. The Marriage Ceremony
13. The Blessing Ceremony for The Deceased
14. The Ancestral Ceremony
15. The Enlightened Buddha Ceremony
16. The Uposatha Ceremony (Reciting Precepts)

With regard to mindful chanting, we take sources from the sacred book, Chanting from the Heart: Buddhist Ceremonies and Daily Practices of Thích Nhất Hạnh. In the field of the Pureland School, we have taken material from the above Vietnamese scripture, "Nghi Lễ Hàng Ngày," and translated it into English.

We should chant at least once a week, any place and any time, or more often if we have more time. The chant will help to avoid negative thoughts, defilements, distractions -any of the myriad things that intrude into the one-pointed mind. We definitely feel the connectedness with Dharma (the Buddha's teaching), we feel the spirit being lifted up, the awakening and the settling of the mind to enter meditation. We will become bright, enduring, detached, diligent, generous, loving, understanding and so on . . . because we practice following the chanting and the role model of Buddhas.

Chanting out loud or silently listening to chanting can also be very relaxing as we go about our day. It can be used to calm our mind before work or sleeping.

For the sake of all the general practitioners, there are some changes, combinations, additions, reductions, and creations made in this English version. This is the first time that both traditions have been combined in an English version for the necessary needs at Huong Sen Buddhist Temple.

We would like to gratefully acknowledge with special thanks the Buddhas, Boddhisattvas, Sanghas, the English translators, Master Thích Nhất Hạnh, our Late Respectful Teacher - Venerable Elder Bhikkhunī Hải Triều Âm and others. You all provided us the awakening words to remind and guide us in the right way of practice. We will keep chanting, learning and practicing it until we and all beings get the enlightenment as well as realize our Buddha nature.

If there is any merit in compiling this book, may it be shared with all sentient beings. May they diligently practice and soon gain the way of love and understanding.

Reciting the sutras, practicing the way of awareness
gives rise to benefits without limit.
We vow to share the fruits with all beings.
We vow to offer tribute to parents, teachers, friends,
and numerous beings who
give guidance and support along the path.
(Thích Nhất Hạnh)

Hương Sen Temple, Riverside, California
March 15, 2023
Bhikkhunī TN Giới Hương

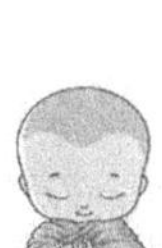

THE RITUAL OFFERING FOOD TO HUNGRY GHOSTS

At the Buddhist temple, every afternoon, this ritual is chanted to offer food to the hungry ghosts and the deceased. It is one of the main rites for the ordained. We should set up a altar with the Amitabha or Mogalanasa statue, flowers, fruit, candles, incense stick, rice gruel, uncooked rice grains, salt, and drinking water, etc... to perform this ritual.

1. Introduction (guidance)
2. The incense offering
3. Salutation
    a. Gratitude the Buddhas and Bodhisattvas
    b. Gratitude the Buddhas in the past
    c. Gratitude the Arahats
    d. Gratitude the Ancestors
4. The repentance and aspiration
5. Opening verse for ghosts
6. Invitation Boddhisattvas & ghosts coming
7. Verse of offering food
8. The Amitabha Sutra (if you have the time)
9. The insight that brings us to the other shore

10. Invoking the Boddhisattvas' names
11. Read the Names of the Buddhas and Bodhisattvas
12. Taking refuge in the Amitabha Buddha
13. May the day and the night be well
14. Prayer for the deceased
15. Salutation thousands of Buddhas in three times
16. Taking refuge at three jewels
17. Sharing the merit & verse for closing
18. The divine gatha.

***

1. INTRODUCTION

Leader: **Today, we** (the leader...) **and sangha... at the...** (the place) **have gathered to organize the ritual offering food to ghosts.**

We recite the Amitabha sutras, invoke the Buddhas' and Bodhisattvas' names, make offerings, and transfer the merits to twelve kinds of souls with names or unnamed including our ancestors and parents in the past, the heroic warriors sacrificed for the country, the deceased died in rivers, accidents and other reasons. May all of them overcome the suffering ocean of the bad karma and be peaceful at the Pure land and

practice with Buddhas and Bodhisattvas.

Please let us be aware of our present and the good fortune we have to be together today, offering all our love and support to the ghosts and to each other during these profound moments of transformation.

Namo Amitabha Buddhaya. (ooo)

2. THE INCENSE OFFERING

Leader: **In gratitude, we offer this incense to all Buddhas and Bodhisattvas throughout space and time.**

May it be fragrant as Earth herself, reflecting our careful efforts, our wholehearted mindfulness, and the fruit of understanding, slowly ripening.

May we and all beings be companions of Buddhas and Bodhisattvas.

May we awaken from forgetfulness and realize our true home. (o)

Namo Offering the Incense
Bodhisattva Mahasattvas. (3 times) (ooo)

3. SALUTATION IN GRATITUDE

(All Sangha members read)

3.1. GRATITUDE THE BUDDHAS AND

<u>BODHISATTVAS:</u>

1. **Offering light in the Ten Directions, the Buddha, the Dharma, and the Sangha, to whom we bow in gratitude.** (o) (1 prostration)
2. **Teaching and living the way of awareness in the very midst of suffering and confusion, Shakyamuni Buddha, the Fully Enlightened One, to whom we bow in gratitude.** (o) (1 prostration)
3. **Cutting through ignorance, awakening our hearts and our minds, Manjushri, the Bodhisattva of Great Understanding, to whom we bow in gratitude.** (o) (1 prostration)
4. **Working mindfully, working joyfully for the sake of all beings, Samantabhadra, the Bodhisattva of Great Action, to whom we bow in gratitude.** (o) (1 prostration)
5. **Seed of awakening and loving kindness in children and all beings, Maitreya, the Buddha to-be-born, to whom we bow in gratitude.** (o) (1 prostration)
6. **Seeing the Buddha in everyone, Sadaparibhuta, the Bodhisattva of Constant Respect, to whom we bow in gratitude.** (o) (1 prostration)
7. **Showing the way fearlessly and compassionately, the stream of all our Ancestral Teachers, to whom we bow in**

gratitude. (ooo) (1 prostration)

3.2. GRATITUDE THE BUDDHAS IN THE PAST

1. **The Buddha Vipashyin, to whom we bow in gratitude.** (o) (1 prostration)
2. **The Buddha Shikhin, to whom we bow in gratitude.** (o) (1 prostration)

   The Buddha Vishvabhu, to whom we bow in gratitude. (o) (1 prostration)
3. **The Buddha Krakkucchandha, to whom we bow in gratitude.** (o) (1 prostration)
4. **The Buddha Konagamana, to whom we bow in gratitude.** (o) (1 prostration)
5. **The Buddha Kashyapa, to whom we bow in gratitude.** (o) (1 prostration)
6. **The Buddha Shakyamuni, to whom we bow in gratitude.** (o) (1 prostration)
7. **The Bodhisattva of Great Understanding, Manjushri, to whom we bow in gratitude.** (o) (1 prostration)
8. **The Bodhisattva of Great Action, Samantabhadra, to whom we bow in gratitude.** (o) (1 prostration)
9. **The Bodhisattva of Great Compassion, Avalokiteshvara, to whom we bow in gratitude.**

(ooo) (1 prostration)

10. **The Bodhisattva of the Great Vow, Kshitigarbha, to whom we bow in gratitude.** (ooo) (1 prostration)

3.3. GRATITUDE THE ARAHATS

1. **The Venerable Kashyapa, to whom we bow in gratitude.** (o) (1 prostration)
2. **The Venerable Shariputra, to whom we bow in gratitude.** (o) (1 prostration)
3. **The Venerable Maudgalyayana, to whom we bow in gratitude.** (o) (1 prostration)
4. **The Venerable Upali, to whom we bow in gratitude.** (o) (1 prostration)
5. **The Venerable Ananda, to whom we bow in gratitude.** (ooo) (1 prostration)

3.4. GRATITUDE THE ANCESTORS

1. **Mother of Buddhas, Bodhisattvas, and all beings, nourishing, holding, and healing all, Bodhisattva Gaia, Great Mother Earth, precious jewel of the cosmos, to whom we bow in gratitude.** (o) (1 prostration)
2. **Radiating light in all directions, source of life on Earth, Mahavairocana Tathagata, Great**

Father Sun, Buddha of infinite light and life, to whom we bow in gratitude. (o) (1 prostration)

3. **Seed of awakening and loving kindness in children and all beings, Maitreya, the Buddha to-be-born, to whom we bow in gratitude.** (o) (1 prostration)
4. **Showing the way fearlessly and compassionately, the stream of all our Ancestral Teachers, to whom we bow in gratitude.** (ooo) (1 prostration)

4. REPENTANCE AND ASPIRATION

Practitioners of the Way have acted unskillfully
with craving, hatred, and ignorance
manifested in actions of body, speech, and mind.
All practitioners repent of this. (o)
Beings of all species have acted unskillfully
with craving, hatred, and ignorance
manifested in actions of body, speech, and mind.
All beings of all species repent of this. (o)
Hungry ghosts have acted unskillfully
with craving, hatred, and ignorance
manifested in actions of body, speech, and mind.
All hungry ghosts repent of this. (o)

Countless beings, I vow to save.

Ceaseless afflictions, I vow to end.

Limitless Dharma Doors, I vow to open.

I vow to realize the highest path of Awakening. (o)

The true nature of beings, I vow to save.

The true nature of afflictions, I vow to end.

The true nature of Dharma Doors, I vow to open.

I vow to realize the true nature of the highest path of Awakening. (o)

Namo Shakyamuni Buddha. (3 times) (ooo)

5. OPENING VERSE FOR GHOSTS

As if a fire is raging on all four sides,

a hungry ghost ceaselessly suffers from heat.

Hungry ghosts, now to be born in a Pure Land,

hear this gatha transmitted by Buddha:

Those who aspire to see and understand

the Buddhas who are present in the Three Times

must always observe that, in the nature of the Dharmadhatu,

all that is arises from the mind. (o)

Namo King Controlling
the Hell Fire Bodhisattva. (3 times) (ooo)

6. INVITATION BODDHISATTVAS & GHOSTS COMING

(This inviting ritual is used for the great requiem ceremony)

i. Light radiates out into the realms of darkness.

We know the Buddha is present at this Requiem Ceremony:

We pray to the Enlightened One to help all the deceased come to the Pure Land, arriving in the Land of Great Bliss, sitting on the lotus flowers.

Homage to the Bodhisattva of Rebirth in the Pure Land. (o)

ii. With flowers and incense, we invite with all our heart

The great KSITIGARBHA BODHISATTVA,

who in the past made the vow

that until the last living being is brought to the other shore

and until all of hell is emptied,

he will not rest and enjoy the fruit of Buddhahood.

Please do not forget your vow, and be present today, participating in this Requiem Ceremony.

iii. With flowers and incense, we invite with all our heart:

The great AVALOKITESHVARA

BODHISATTVA,

the One who practices deep compassionate listening,

the One who is always ready to come to where he is needed,

the One who brings the boat of compassion to rescue living beings drowning in the Ocean of Suffering.

Please do not forget your vow, and be present today, participating in this Requiem Ceremony.

iv. With flowers and incense, we invite with all our heart.

In the immense Ocean of Suffering,

each living being carries his or her own karma.

Those of you who have not had a chance to wake up from your long dream, begin to practice calling the name of the Buddha in order to leave behind the shore of Delusion and come to the land of Bliss.

THIS IS THE FIRST INCENSE OFFERING.

This is the initial invitation:

Relying on the spiritual power of the Buddhas, the Dharma,

and the Sangha, and of the powerful dharanis,

our ancestors of the past seven generations, all deceased
members of our great family, and every wandering ghost are summoned here tonight to participate in the Offering and Requiem Ceremony, to listen to the Dharma and enjoy the food, the drink, and the nourishing, transforming, and healing nectar of compassion offered tonight.

v. With flowers and incense, we invite with all our heart.

The sun has just set,
The moon is beginning to rise.
Although we do not see you in the forms we used to see,
we know you are there in new forms.

THIS IS THE SECOND INCENSE OFFERING.

This is the second invitation:
Relying on the spiritual power of the Buddhas, the Dharma,
and the Sangha, and of the powerful dharanis,

our ancestors
of the past seven generations, all deceased members of our
great family, and every wandering ghost are summoned here
tonight to participate in the Offering and Requiem Ceremony,
to listen to the Dharma and enjoy the food, the drink, and the
nourishing, transforming, and healing nectar of compassion
offered tonight.

vi. With flowers and incense, we invite with all our heart.

All formations are like dreams,
no one escapes impermanence,
but thanks to the power of the Three Jewels,
we always have a way out of birth and death.

THIS IS THE THIRD INCENSE OFFERING.

This is the third invitation:
Relying on the spiritual power of the Buddhas, the Dharma,
and the Sangha, and of the powerful dharanis,
our ancestors of the past seven generations, all deceased

members of our great family, and every wandering ghost
are summoned here tonight to participate in the Offering and
Requiem Ceremony, to listen to the Dharma and enjoy the
food, the drink, and the nourishing, transforming, and healing
nectar of compassion offered tonight.

vii. After reciting the mantras and dharanis we invite

everyone who has awakened and has heard.
May the energy of the Three Jewels protect everyone.
Everyone who is able to come to the ceremony, please come when you have heard us.

viii. You have heard our invitation and have come.

Everyone is invited to be served with the nectar of immortality.
Everyone is invited to sit down peacefully to listen to the holy
scriptures.
May the Dharma transform all afflictions and bring back joy and
freedom.

Please listen to the wonderful teaching on Emptiness.

Namo the Great Vow Kshitigarbha

Bodhisattva Mahasattva. (3 times) (ooo)

7. VERSE OF OFFERING FOOD

Homage to the Tathagata Multiple Jewel. (o)
Homage to the Tathagata Jewel Victory. (o)
Homage to the Tathagata Wonderful Form Body. (o)
Homage to the Tathagata Extensive Body. (o)
Homage to the Tathagata Far from Fear. (o)
Homage to the Tathagata of the nectar of compassion. (o)
Homage to the Tathagata of Infinite Light. (o)

Maintaining our concentration, we purify this offering of food.
So too in practitioners throughout the Ten Directions.
May they all be satisfied, letting go of craving, moving out of darkness to be born into a Pure Land.
May they truly take refuge in the Three Jewels, give rise to Awakened Mind, and realize the highest path.
For the benefit of practitioners, may the merit

of the practice
form the ground on which the future Buddha stands. (o)

Maintaining our concentration, we purify this offering of food.
So too in all species throughout the Ten Directions.
May they all be satisfied, letting go of craving, moving out of darkness to be born into a Pure Land.
May they truly take refuge in the Three Jewels, give rise to Awakened Mind, and realize the highest path.
For the benefit of all species, may the merit of the practice
form the ground on which the future Buddha stands. (o)

Maintaining our concentration, we purify this offering of food.
So too in hungry ghosts throughout the Ten Directions.
May they all be satisfied, letting go of craving, moving out of darkness to be born into a Pure Land.
May they truly take refuge in the Three Jewels, give rise to Awakened Mind, and realize the highest path.

For the benefit of hungry ghosts, may the merit of the practice
form the ground on which the future Buddha stands. (o)

Practitioners of the Way,
we make offerings of food
multiplied in Ten Directions
so that you can all receive them.
By the merit of this offering,
may we and all practitioners
be successful in the realization of the path. (o)

Beings of all species,
we make offerings of food
multiplied in Ten Directions
so that you can all receive them.
By the merit of this offering,
may we and all species
be successful in the realization of the path. (o)

Hungry ghosts,
we make offerings of food
multiplied in Ten Directions
so that you can all receive them.
By the merit of this offering,
may we and all hungry ghosts
be successful in the realization of the path. (o)

Namo the Great Vow Kshitigarbha Bodhisattva Mahasattva. (3 times) (ooo)

8. THE AMITABHA SUTRA

[1] MEETING AT JETA GROVE

Thus, have I heard. At one time the Bhagavat was staying in Jeta Grove monastery in Anathapindada's Garden at Shravasti, together with a large company of twelve hundred and fifty monks, who were all venerable shravakas and well-known great arhats. They were headed by eminent shravakas, such as the Venerable Shariputra, Mahamaudgalyayana, Mahakashyapa and Aniruddha. He was also accompanied by innumerable bodhisattvas, mahasattvas, who were all dwelling in the Stage of Non-retrogression and were adorned with immeasurable merits and virtues, headed by great bodhisattvas, such as Bodhisattva Manjushri, Bodhisattva Ajita, Bodhisattva Nityodyukta and Bodhisattva Anikshipta-dhura. Also in the assembly were a hundred thousand kotis of nayutas [of devas] headed by Shakra along with the King of Mahabrahma Heaven, the Lord of Saha world, as well as the Four Guardian Kings and others. Many demi-gods, innumerable heavenly and human beings, asuras

and others assembled and took their seats to hear the Dharma.

[2] INTRODUCTION THE BUDDHA-LANDS

The Bhagavat said to Shariputra: "Do you know that if you travel westwards from here, passing a hundred thousand kotis of nayutas of Buddha-lands, you come to the land called 'Utmost Bliss,' where there is a Bhagavat named 'Amitayus' or 'Amitabha' with ten titles, including Tathagata, Arhat and Samyaksambuddha. He is living there at this very moment, teaching the profound and wonderful Dharma to sentient beings to give them supreme benefit and bliss.

[3] THE SOLEMN PURELAND

Why, Shariputra, is that land called 'Utmost Bliss'? Shariputra, beings in that land suffer no afflictions and pain but experience only pure immeasurable joy and happiness. For this reason, that land is called 'Utmost Bliss.'

Again, Shariputra, in the pure Buddha-land of Utmost Bliss there are seven rows of jewelled balustrades, seven rows of jewelled tala-trees, and sevenfold jewelled nets, which surround everywhere and are completely decorated with four jewels, namely, gold, silver, beryl and

crystal. Shariputra, that Buddha-land is full of such glorious adornments of supreme qualities, which are most pleasing to the mind. For this reason, that land is called 'Utmost Bliss.'

Again, Shariputra, in the pure Buddha-land of Utmost Bliss here and there are many seven-jewelled ponds filled with water of eight excellent qualities, namely, (1) pure, (2) cool, (3) sweet-tasting, (4) soft, (5) moistening, (6) comforting, (7) quenching thirst, hunger and many other needs, and (8) nourishing the senses, increasing the activites of the four elements and producing superior goodness. Sentient beings with a large stock of merits always enjoy using such water. The bottom of these ponds is lined with gold sand, and from the four sides of each pond rise stairs made of the four jewels, most pleasing to the mind. Marvellous jewelled trees surrounding the ponds are evenly spaced, scented with rich fragrance and decorated with the seven delightful jewels, namely, gold, silver, beryl, crystal, rosy pearls, cornelian and sapphire.

In the ponds, at all times, lotuses of various colours as large as chariot-wheels are in bloom. Blue flowers radiate blue light, brilliance and splendor; yellow ones radiate yellow light, brilliance and splendor; red ones radiate red light, brilliance and splendour; white ones

radiate white light, brilliance and splendor; four-coloured ones radiate four-coloured light, brilliance and splendor. Shariputra, that Buddha-land is full of such glorious adornments of supreme qualities, which are most pleasing to the mind. For this reason, that land is called 'Utmost Bliss.'

Again, Shariputra, in that pure Buddha-land of Utmost Bliss limitless exquisite music is spontaneously played at all times. The sound is harmonious and most pleasant to hear. When sentient beings hear its excellent sound, their evil passions are completely removed, numerous good acts multiply, and they soon attain the highest perfect Enlightenment. Shariputra, that Buddha-land is full of such glorious adornments of supreme qualities, which are most pleasing to the mind. For this reason, that land is called 'Utmost Bliss.'

Again, Shariputra, the ground throughout that pure Buddha-land of Utmost Bliss is of true gold. It is soft to the touch and refreshing, shining boundlessly and adorned with rare jewels. Shariputra, that Buddha-land is full of such glorious adornments of supreme qualities, which are most pleasing to the mind. For this reason, that land is called 'Utmost Bliss.'

Again, Shariputra, in that pure Buddha-land

of Utmost Bliss, six times during the day and night, various heavenly blossoms of rare beauty continuously rain down from the sky. They are brilliant and refreshing, soft and variegated, pleasing to the mind and the senses. They do not rouse greedy attachment, but increase countless inconceivable merits in sentient beings. Six times during the day and night, the beings in that land offer those blossoms to Amitayus in homage. Every morning they take those heavenly blossoms and, in such a short time it takes for a meal, fly to innumerable other lands to pay homage to a hundred, thousand kotis of Buddhas. They offer to each Buddha a hundred thousand kotis of such blossoms and return home to the Pure Land, as if to enjoy leisure in a heavenly abode. Shariputra, that Buddha-land is full of such glorious adornments of supreme qualities, which are most pleasing to the mind. For this reason, that land is called 'Utmost Bliss.'

Again, Shariputra, in that pure Buddha-land of Utmost Bliss there are always many rare species of beautiful birds of various colours, such as swams, geese, herons, storks, cranes, peacocks, parrots, kalavinkas and jivamjivakas. Six times during the day and night, those birds form a flock and sing with melodious and delicate tones, producing diverse sounds to proclaim numerous wonderful teachings, such as the [four] mindful acts, the [four] ways of stopping evils, the [four] miraculous powers, the [five] roots of goodness, the [five] powers, the [seven] factors of wisdom, and the [Eightfold] Noble Path. Having heard their singing, the sentient beings in that land gain innumerable merits through mindfulness of the Buddha, Dharma and Sangha, and their bodies long retain the perfume of virtue. Shariputra, do you think that the birds in that land belong to the evil realm of animals? Do not hold such a view! The reason is that none of the three evil realms, not even their names, exist in that Buddha's Pure Land; how much less should there be real birds belonging to the realm of animals born as retribution for evil karma? You should know that they are manifestations created by Amitayus so that they can proclaim innumerable sounds of the Dharma to give benefit and bliss to sentient beings. Shariputra, that Buddha-land is full of such wonderful glorious adornments, which are most pleasing to the mind. For this reason, that land is called 'Utmost Bliss.'

Again, Shariputra, in that pure Buddha-land of Utmost Bliss soft breezes always blow. When they waft through the jewelled trees and jewelled nets, wonderful sounds are produced. As if a hundred thousand kotis of celestial musical instruments were playing together to produce exquisite sounds, when soft breezes which constantly arise in that land waft through the jewelled trees and jewelled nets, they produce various excellent sounds, which proclaim many teachings of the Dharma. Having heard those sounds, sentient beings in that land give rise to numerous meritorious acts, such as mindfulness of the Buddha, Dharma and Sangha. Shariputra, that Buddha-land is full of such glorious adornments of supreme qualities, which are most pleasing to the mind. For this reason, that land is called 'Utmost Bliss.'

Shariputra, in that pure Buddha-land of Utmost Bliss there are wonderful manifestations such as those, which are innumerable and inconceivable. Even if a hundred thousand kotis of nayutas of innumerable tongues should praise their excellent qualities for a hundred thousand kotis of nayutas of kalpas, each tongue producing immeasurable voices, they would not be able to praise them to the full. For this reason, [that land] is called the Land of Utmost Bliss.

[4] INTRODUCTION THE AMITABHA BUDDHA

Again, Shariputra, why is the Buddha of the pure Buddha-land of Utmost Bliss called 'Amitayus'? Because, Shariputra, the life-span

of that Tathagata and all beings living there last for immeasurable and innumerable great kalpas, the Tathagata of that land is called 'Amitayus.' Shariputra, why is the Buddha also called 'Amitabha'? Shariputra, the Tathagata always emits boundless and innumerable rays of glorious light, illuminating all the Buddha-lands of the ten directions without hindrance, so as to display Buddhist activities. For this reason, the Tathagata of that land is called 'Amitabha.' Shariputra, the Pure Land of that Buddha is full of such glorious adornments, which are most pleasing to the mind. For this reason, that land is called 'Utmost Bliss.'

Again, Shariputra, the Buddha Amitayus of that pure Buddha-land of Utmost Bliss always has shravaka disciples, all of them arhats, who are possessed of various excellent merits and whose number is unlimited and incalculable. Shariputra, the Pure Land of that Buddha is full of such glorious adornments, which are most pleasing to the mind. For this reason, that land is called 'Utmost Bliss.'

Again, Shariputra, the Buddha Amitayus of that pure Buddha-land of Utmost Bliss always has innumerable bodhisattva disciples, all of them in the Stage of Becoming a Buddha after One More Life. They are possessed of various

excellent merits, and their number is unlimited and incalculable. Even if one praised their merits for innumerable kalpas, one would not be able to praise them fully. Shariputra, that Buddha-land is filled with such glorious adornments, which are most pleasing to the mind. For this reason, that land is called 'Utmost Bliss.'

[5] THE GREAT CAUSE TO BE BORN IN THE UTMOST BLISSFUL LAND

Again, Shariputra, sentient beings born in that land all dwell in the Stage of Non-retrogression, and will not fall again into an evil realm, be born in a border-land or in the state of debased people or mlecchas. They always enjoy visiting pure lands of other Buddhas. With their excellent vows and practice advancing and developing every moment, they will unfailingly realize the highest, perfect Enlightenment. Shariputra, that Buddha-land is full of such glorious merits, which are most pleasing to the mind. For this reason, that land is called 'Utmost Bliss.'

Again, Shariputra, if sentient beings hear of the glorious manifestations of countless merits in that pure Buddha-land of Amitayus, they should all awaken aspiration to be born there. The reasons are: first, those born there will meet those Great Beings adorned with such countless

merits as mentioned above; second, they will enjoy the pleasure of the Mahayana Dharma intrinsic to this pure Buddha-land adorned with such innumerable merits; and third, with their own immeasurable vows and practice advancing and developing every moment, they will quickly realize the highest perfect Enlightenment. Shariputra, those who are to be born in that Buddha-land do not have few but already countless and unlimited merits, so such sentient beings can attain birth in the pure Buddha-land of Utmost Bliss of the Buddha Amitayus.

Again, Shariputra, if good men or women of pure faith, having heard Amitayus Buddha's name of innumerable, boundless and inconceivable merits and also heard of the glorious adornments of the Land of Utmost Bliss, concentrate their thoughts on them with undistracted mind even for one day, two days, three, four, five, six or seven days, then, at the hour of death, Amitayus, surrounded by innumerable shravaka disciples and bodhisattvas, will appear before those good men or women and give them compassionate protection to keep their minds from falling into confusion. Thus, after death, following the Buddha Amitayus and his retinue, they will be born in his Pure Land of Utmost Bliss.

Shariputra, as I perceive that such blissful

benefits are matters of great importance, I pronounce these words of truth: Good men and good women of pure faith who hear Amitayus Buddha's name of inconceivable merits and also learn of the pure Buddha-land of Utmost Bliss should all receive [the teaching] in faith, arouse aspiration, practise the method as prescribed, and attain birth in that Buddha-land.

[6] SIX DIRECTIONS ALL PRAISED THE BUDDHA LANDS

Shariputra, just as I praise the innumerable, unlimited and inconceivable merits of the Buddha-land of Amitayus, so do the Buddhas of the eastern direction as numerous as the sands of the Ganges, such as Aksobhya Tathagata, Meru-dhvaja Tathagata, Mahameru Tathagata, Meru-prabhasa Tathagata, and Manju-dhvaja Tathagata. While dwelling in their own pure lands of the east, they extend their long, broad tongues and, encompassing with them the universe of a thousand million worlds, pronounce these words of truth: Sentient beings should all receive in faith this gate of the Dharma concerning praise of the inconceivable merits of the Buddha-land and protection by all Buddhas.

[7] THE SOUTH

Again, Shariputra, there are in the southern direction Buddhas as numerous as the sands of the Ganges, such as Candra-surya-pradipa Tathagata, Yashah-prabha Tathagata, Maharci-skandha Tathagata, Meru-pradipa Tathagata and Ananta-virya Tathagata. While dwelling in their own pure lands of the south, they extend their long, broad tongues and, encompassing with them the universe of a thousand million worlds, pronounce these words of truth: Sentient beings should all receive in faith this gate of the Dharma concerning praise of the inconceivable merits of the Buddha-land and protection by all Buddhas.

[8] THE WEST

Again, Shariputra, there are in the western direction Buddhas as numerous as the sands of the Ganges, such as Amitayus Tathagata, Amita-skandha Tathagata, Amita-prabha Tathagata, Amita-dhvaja Tathagata, Maheshvara Tathagata, Mahaprabha Tathagata, Jvalana Tathagata, Maharatna-ketu Tathagata and Sphuta-rashmi Tathagata. While dwelling in their own pure lands of the west, they extend their long, broad tongues and, encompassing with them the universe of a thousand million worlds, pronounce these words of truth: Sentient beings should all receive in faith

this gate of the Dharma concerning praise of the inconceivable merits of the Buddha-land and protection by all Buddhas.

[9] THE NORTH

Again, Shariputra, there are in the northern direction Buddhas as numerous as the sands of the Ganges, such as Amita-prabha-vyuha-abhijna- buddhi Tathagata, Mahaskandha Tathagata, Amita-divya-dundubhi-vaishvanara-nirghosa Tathagata, Jaleni-prabha Tathagata and Salendra-raja Tathagata. While dwelling in their own pure lands of the north, they extend their long, broad tongues and, encompassing with them the universe of a thousand million worlds, pronounce these words of truth: Sentient beings should all receive in faith this gate of the Dharma concerning praise of the inconceivable merits of the Buddha-land and protection by all Buddhas.

[10] THE NADIR

Again, Shariputra, there are in the nadir Buddhas as numerous as the sands of the Ganges, such as Sarva-saddharma-darshana-yukti-sada-jvalana- rajottama-shri-prabha Tathagata, Simha Tathagata, Yashas Tathagata, Yashah-prabhasa Tathagata, Dharma Tathagata,

Saddharma Tathagata, Dharma-dhvaja Tathagata, Guna-mitra Tathagata and Guna-nama Tathagata. While dwelling in their own pure lands of the nadir, they extend their long, broad tongues and, encompassing with them the universe of a thousand million worlds, pronounce these words of truth: Sentient beings should all receive in faith this Dharma-gate expounding praise of the inconceivable merits of the Buddha-land and protection by all Buddhas.

[11] THE ZENITH

Again, Shariputra, there are in the zenith Buddhas as numerous as the sands of the Ganges, such as Brahma-ghosa Tathagata, Naksatra-raja Tathagata, Gandha-prabhasa Tathagata, Utpala-shri-kalpa Tathagata and Sarvartha-darsha Tathagata. While dwelling in their own pure lands of the zenith, they extend their long, broad tongues and, encompassing with them the universe of a thousand million worlds, pronounce these words of truth: Sentient beings should all receive in faith this gate of the Dharma concerning praise of the inconceivable merits of the Buddha-land and protection by all Buddhas.

[12] THE SOUTH-EASTERN

Again, Shariputra, there are in the south-eastern direction Buddhas as numerous as the sands of the Ganges, such as Uttama-vipula-megha-ghosa-raja Tathagata. While dwelling in their own pure lands of the south-east, they extend their long, broad tongues and, encompassing with them the universe of a thousand million worlds, pronounce these words of truth: Sentient beings should all receive in faith this gate of the Dharma concerning praise of the inconceivable merits of the Buddha-land and protection by all Buddhas.

[13] THE SOUTH-WESTERN

Again, Shariputra, there are in the south-western direction Buddhas as numerous as the sands of the Ganges, such as Uttama-surya-prabha-yasho-guna Tathagata. While dwelling in their own pure lands of the south-west, they extend their long, broad tongues and, encompassing with them the universe of a thousand million worlds, pronounce these words of truth: Sentient beings should all receive in faith this gate of the Dharma concerning praise of the inconceivable merits of the Buddha-land and protection by all Buddhas.

[14] THE NORTH-WESTERN

Again, Shariputra, there are in the north-western direction Buddhas as numerous as the sands of the Ganges, such as Amita-guna-jvalanadhipati-prabhasa Tathagata. While dwelling in their own pure lands of the north-west, they extend their long, broad tongues and, encompassing with them the universe of a thousand million worlds, pronounce these words of truth: Sentient beings should all receive in faith this gate of the Dharma concerning praise of the inconceivable merits of the Buddha-land and protection by all Buddhas.

[15] THE NORTH-EASTERN

Again, Shariputra, there are in the north-eastern direction Buddhas as numerous as the sands of the Ganges, such as Asamkhya-shata-sahasra-koti- nayuta-vipula-buddhi Tathagata. While dwelling in their own pure lands of the north-east, they extend their long, broad tongues and, encompassing with them the universe of a thousand million worlds, pronounce these words of truth: Sentient beings should all receive in faith this gate of the Dharma concerning praise of the inconceivable merits of the Buddha-land and protection by all Buddhas.

[16] THE INCONCEIVABLE MERIT OF THE AMITABHA SUTRA

Shariputra, why is this sutra named 'the Dharma-gate expounding praise of the inconceivable merits of the Buddha-land and protection by all Buddhas? Shariputra, it is revealed in this sutra that the inconceivable merits of Amitayus Buddha's Land of Utmost Bliss are praised and glorified and that all Buddhas, Bhagavats, of the ten directions, while dwelling in their own lands, display glorious and wonderful manifestations and pronounce words of truth, urging sentient beings to receive this teaching in faith, in order to guide and benefit them and give them peace and bliss. For this reason, this sutra is called 'the gate of the Dharma concerning praise of the inconceivable merits of the Buddha-land and protection by all Buddhas.'

Shariputra, if good men or women, who have heard this sutra, now hear or will hear it, have already awakened or will awaken deep faith, they are embraced by those Buddhas, Bhagavats, dwelling in the ten directions, as numerous as ten times the number of the sands of the Ganges. All who practise as prescribed will not regress but will definitely attain the highest perfect Enlightenment and be born in the Pure Land of Utmost Bliss of Amitayus. For this reason,

Shariputra, all sentient beings should receive in faith and understand well my words and the words of the Buddhas, Bhagavats, of the ten directions, and should make great efforts and diligently practise as prescribed. Do not allow any doubt to arise.

Again, Shariputra, if good men or women have already aspired or will aspire or now aspire to the glorious adornments in the Pure Land of Utmost Bliss of Amitayus, they will be definitely embraced by those Buddhas, Bhagavats, dwelling in the ten directions, as numerous as the sands of the Ganges, even ten times that number. All who practise as prescribed will not regress but will definitely attain the highest perfect Enlightenment and be born in the Pure Land of Utmost Bliss of Amitayus. For this reason, Shariputra, good men and women of pure faith should all believe deeply in Amitayus Buddha's Pure Land of Utmost Bliss and aspire to be born there. Do not be indolent.

[17] THE AMITABHA SUTRA IS THE MOST DIFFICULT FOR THE WORLD TO ACCEPT

Shariputra, just as I now praise and glorify the inconceivable merits of Amitayus Buddha's Land of Utmost Bliss, all other Buddhas, Bhagavats, of the ten directions likewise praise my boundless inconceivable merits, saying: 'How marvellous it is that Shakyamuni, Shakya Dharma-King, Tathagata, Arthat, Samyaksambuddha, Possessed of Wisdom and Practice, Sugata, Knower of the World, the Unsurpassed, Tamer of Men, Teacher of Gods and Humans, Buddha and Bhagavat, has appeared in this Saha world during the period of the five corruptions: namely, those of time, sentient beings, passions, views and life-span, and that, having attained the highest perfect Enlightenment, delivered this teaching, most difficult for the world to accept, in order to guide and benefit sentient beings and give them peace and bliss.'

Thus, Shariputra, you should know that I have appeared in this Saha world of various defilements during the period of the five corruptions and, having attained the highest perfect Enlightenment, delivered this teaching, most difficult for the world to accept, in order to guide and benefit sentient beings and give them peace and bliss. This is indeed a rare and marvellous task, which is beyond comprehension.

"If, Shariputra, there are good men or women of pure faith who, having heard this teaching, most difficult for the world to accept, receive it in faith, uphold and expound it to others, and practise it as prescribed, you should know that

such people are extremely rare. In the past they have planted roots of goodness in the presence of innumerable Buddhas. After death they will surely be born in the Western Land of Utmost Bliss, where they will enjoy various glorious adornments and the pleasure of Mahayana Dharma embodied in the Buddha's Pure Land. They can approach Amitayus Buddha and make offerings to him six times during the day and night. They can also fly to [the lands in] the ten directions to make offerings to Buddhas, where they will hear the Dharma taught by them and will receive assurances of their attainment of Buddhahood. Thus they will be able to perfect quickly the merits and wisdom and realize the highest perfect Enlightenment."

[18] SUPPORTED BY INNUMERABLE DEVAS, HUMANS, ASURAS & THE DHARMA PROTECTIVE DEITIES

When the Bhavagat had delivered this sutra, all the great shravakas, such as the Venerable Shariputra, and bodhisattvas, mahasattvas, together with all beings, including innumerable devas, humans and asuras, greatly rejoiced at the Buddha's exposition and received it in faith./.

(Translated on Imperial Order by Tripitaka Master Hsuan-tsang of Great T'ang Dynasty translated from Chinese by Hisao Inagaki)

9. THE INSIGHT THAT BRINGS US TO THE OTHER SHORE

The Heart of Prajnaparamita (Perfect Wisdom)

Avalokiteshvara while practicing deeply with the Insight that Brings Us to the Other Shore, suddenly discovered that all of the five Skandhas are equally empty, and with this realization he overcame all Ill-being (suffering). (o)

Listen Sariputra, this Body itself is Emptiness and Emptiness itself is this Body.
This Body is not other than Emptiness and Emptiness is not other than this Body.
The same is true of Feelings, Perceptions, Mental Formations, and Consciousness. (o)

Listen Sariputra, all phenomena bear the mark of Emptiness; their true nature is the nature of neither Birth nor Death, neither Being nor Non-being, neither Defilement nor Purity, neither Increasing nor Decreasing. (o)

That is why in Emptiness, Body, Feelings, Perceptions, Mental Formations and

Consciousness are not separate self-entities. The Eighteen Realms of Phenomena which are the six Sense Organs, six Sense Objects, and six Consciousnesses are also not separate self-entities. (o)

The Twelve Links of Interdependent Arising and their Extinction are also not separate self-entities. Ill-being, the Causes of Ill-being, the End of Ill-being, the Path, insight and attainment, are also not separate self-entities. Whoever can see this no longer needs anything to attain. (o)

Bodhisattvas who practice the Insight that Brings Us to the Other Shore see no more obstacles in their mind, and because there are no more obstacles in their mind, they can overcome all fear, destroy all wrong perceptions and realize Perfect Nirvana.

All Buddhas in the past, present and future by practicing the Insight that Brings Us to the Other Shore, are all capable of attaining Authentic and Perfect Enlightenment. (o)

Therefore, Sariputra, it should be known that the Insight that Brings Us to the Other Shore is a Great Mantra, the most illuminating mantra,

the highest mantra, a mantra beyond compare, the True Wisdom that has the power to put an end to all kinds of suffering. (o)
Therefore, let us proclaim a mantra. To praise the Insight that Brings Us to the Other Shore. Gone, gone, gone beyond, gone to the other shore, awake, rejoice! (3 times) (o)

Namo the Great Compassionate Avalokiteshvara Bodhisattva. (3 times) (ooo)

10. INVOKING THE BODHISATTVAS' NAMES

10.1. AVALOKITESHVARA

We invoke your name, Avalokiteshvara. We aspire to learn your way of listening in order to help relieve the suffering in the world. You know how to listen in order to understand. We invoke your name in order to practice listening with all our attention and openheartedness. We will sit and listen without any prejudice. We will sit and listen without judging or reacting.

We will sit and listen in order to understand. We will sit and listen so attentively that we will be able to hear what the other person is saying and also what is being left unsaid. We know that just by listening deeply we already alleviate a great deal of pain and suffering in the other person. (o)

10.2. MANJUSHRI

We invoke your name, Manjushri. We aspire to learn your way, which is to be still and to look deeply into the heart of things and into the hearts of people. We will look with all our attention and openheartedness. We will look with unprejudiced eyes. We will look without judging or reacting. We will look deeply so that we will be able to see and understand the roots of suffering and the impermanent and selfless nature of all that is. We will practice your way of using the sword of understanding to cut through the bonds of suffering, thus freeing ourselves and other species. (o)

10.3. SAMANTABHADRA

We invoke your name, Samantabhadra. We aspire to practice your vow to act with the eyes and heart of compassion, to bring joy to one person in the morning and to ease the pain of one person in the afternoon. We know that the happiness of others is our own happiness, and we aspire to practice joy on the path of service. We know that every word, every look, every action, and every smile can bring happiness to others. We know that if we practice wholeheartedly, we ourselves may become an inexhaustible source of peace and joy for our loved ones and for all species. (o)

10.4. KSHITIGARBHA

We invoke your name, Kshitigarbha. We aspire to learn your way of being present where there is darkness, suffering, oppression, and despair, so we can bring light, hope, relief, and liberation to those places. We are determined not to forget about or abandon those in desperate situations. We will do our best to establish contact with those who cannot find a way out of their suffering, those whose cries for help, justice, equality, and human rights are not being heard. We know that hell can be found in many places on Earth. We will do our best not to contribute to creating more hells on Earth, and we will help transform the hells that already exist. We will practice in order to realize the qualities of perseverance and stability, so that, like the Earth, we can always be supportive and faithful to those in need. (o)

10.5. SADAPARIBHUTA

We invoke your name Sadaparibhuta. We aspire to learn your way of looking deeply with the eyes of nondiscrimination in order to see the virtuous qualities of others. Whenever you meet anyone, you bow respectfully and say in appreciation: I respect you deeply. You are a future Buddha. We vow to look deeply into ourselves to recognize the positive qualities that are there, to accept and

to love ourselves. We vow only to water positive seeds in ourselves and in those around us. Then our thoughts, words, and deeds will give rise to self-confidence and acceptance in ourselves, our children, grandchildren, and all those we know. We vow to look deeply with the eyes of nondiscrimination to see that your joy and success is also our joy and success. We vow to behave and to speak with humility and respect. We vow to practice loving speech to help people who underestimate themselves see that they are wonders of the universe. We know that only when we are able to transcend the barriers of a separate self, shall we be able to transform the superiority, inferiority, and equality complexes and realize true happiness and freedom. (o)

Namo the Great Bodhisattva Mahasattvas.
(3 times) (ooo)

11. READ THE NAMES OF BUDDHAS & BODHISATTVAS

The river of attachment is ten thousand miles long.
The waves on the ocean of confusion stretch so far.
If you wish to go beyond the realms of samsara,
Recollect the Buddha with one pointed mind. (o)
The Pure Land is available in our True Mind.

Amitabha manifests from the true nature of things,

Shining light on the three worlds and the ten directions,

Always abiding in the present moment.

May I go back to Amitabha Buddha,

The founder of the Pure Land,

The source of limitless lifespan.

May I with one heart visualize

And recollect this holy name.

Namo Amitabhaya Buddhaya, the Buddha of Infinite Light. (3 times) (o)

Namo Manjushri, the Bodhisattva of Great Understanding. (3 times) (o)

Namo Samantabhadra, the Bodhisattva of Great Action. (3 times) (o)

Namo Avalokiteshvara, the Bodhisattva of Great Compassion. (3 times) (o)

Namo Kshitigarbhaya Bodhisattvaya, the Bodhisattva of Great Aspiration. (3 times) (o)

12. TAKING REFUGE IN AMITABHA BUDDHA

Taking refuge in the Amitabha Buddha

In the wondrous ultimate dimension,

I devote my heart to returning to myself
And holding to the source of mindfulness.
I have vowed to go for refuge to the Amitabha Buddha. (o)

I bow my head and ask the Buddha
To receive us in his embrace.
As the Pure Land manifests,
Please bring your torch of light
To shine onto my thoughts.
Please bring the boat of long lifespan
To carry my body through life
So I live with peace and joy,
So my aspiration can be fully realized.
Buddha, please always protect me. (o)

Not letting my mind grow slack,
So that I end wrong perceptions
And the affliction fall away.
In the present moment
Buddha can be found in this world.
Taking every step with solidity and freedom
We walk in the Pure Land.

When we live the present moment mindfully,
The Pure Land is already a reality.
So whatever form we take in the future,
We can be assured of peace and joy. (o)

If we are able to recollect the Amitabha
With undispersed, one-pointed mind,
The nine lotus grades will appear.
May we enjoy life for ourselves and others
And know in advance our time of death.
At death may our mind not flinch,
Our body not be sick and in pain,
Our thoughts not waiver. (o)
May the Amitabha and his holy assembly
Holding up the golden lotuses
Be present without delay.
Together may we set out in freedom
May we see the Buddha in the opening lotus.
May the Pure Land be our home.
I bow my head to ask Buddha to be my witness
To my never slackening practice. (o)

Namo Amitabha Buddha (3 times) (ooo)

13. MAY THE DAY & NIGHT BE WELL

May the day be well and the night be well.
May the midday hour bring happiness too.
In every minute and every second, may the day and night be well.
By the blessing of the Triple Gem, may all things be protected and safe.
May all beings born in each of the four ways live in a land of purity.
May all in the Three Realms be born upon Lotus Thrones.
May countless wandering souls realize the three virtuous positions of the Bodhisattva Path.
May all living beings, with grace and ease, fulfill the Bodhisattva Stages.
The countenance of the World-Honored One, like the full moon
or like the orb of the sun, shines with the light of clarity.
A halo of wisdom spreads in every direction, enveloping all with love and compassion, joy and equanimity.

Namo Shakyamunaye Buddhaya. (3 times) (ooo)

14. PRAYER

Namo Amitabha Buddhaya. (o)

Namo the Buddhas, Bodhisattvas and the

Dharma Protective Deities prove (o)

Today, we (the leading Bhikkhuni...) **and sangha... at the** .... (the place...) **have gathered to organize the ritual offering food to ghosts. We recite the Amitabha sutra, invoke the Buddhas' and Bodhisattvas' names, make offerings, and transfer the merits to twelve kinds of souls with names or unname.**

We would like to return this merit to pray for Buddhists... (the full name, the Dharma name, age...) **together with the householders and all Sangha members present here are always healthy, happy and diligent in practice. May all year round be auspicious and joy. May our bodhicitta firm; our wills are steady; and we will gain self-awareness as well as the perfective enlightenment.** (o)

Again, we give back this merit to pray for the deceased... (the full name, the Dharma name, longevity...) **with our ancestors and parents in the past, the heroic warriors sacrificed for the country, the deceased died in rivers, accidents and other reasons. There are twelve kinds of souls with names or unname. May all of them overcome the suffering ocean of the bad karma and be peaceful at the Pure land and practice with Buddhas and Bodhisattvas.**

Finally, may all sentient beings soon complete

the Way of Love and Understanding.

Namo Amitabha Buddhaya. (ooo)

15. SALUTATION THOUSANDS BUDDHAS IN THREE TIMES

There are many the great causes

The ten directions, three lives and realms

I keep my body and mind pure

Pay homage at all without being left behind. (o)

We pay respects sincerely to the four graces of the three realms:

Namo the Buddhas of the kalpa thousands in the past. (o) (1 prostration)

Namo the Buddhas of the kalpa thousands in the present. (o) (1 prostration)

Namo the Buddhas of the kalpa thousands in the future. (o) (1 prostration)

16. TAKING REFUGE AT THREE JEWELS

- I take refuge in the Buddha,

the one who shows me the way in this life.

I take refuge in the Dharma,

the way of understanding and of love.

I take refuge in the Sangha,

the community that lives in harmony and awareness. (o) (1 prostration)

- Dwelling in the refuge of Buddha,

I clearly see the path of light and beauty in the world.

Dwelling in the refuge of Dharma,

I learn to open many doors on the path of transformation.

Dwelling in the refuge of Sangha,

shining light that supports me, keeping my practice free of obstruction. (o) (1 prostration)

-Taking refuge in the Buddha in myself,

I aspire to help all people recognize their own awakened nature,

realizing the Mind of Love.

Taking refuge in the Dharma in myself,

I aspire to help all people fully master the ways of practice

and walk together on the path of liberation.

Taking refuge in the Sangha in myself,

I aspire to help all people build Fourfold

Communities,

to embrace all beings and support their transformation. (ooo) (1 prostration)

17. SHARING THE MERIT & VERSE FOR CLOSING

Reciting the sutras, practicing the way of awareness gives rise to benefits without limit.

We vow to share the fruits with all beings.

We vow to offer tribute to parents, teachers, friends, and numerous beings who give guidance and support along the path. (o)

May we be born now in the Pure Land

within the heart of a lotus flower.

In the moment when the lotus blooms,

we touch the reality of no-birth and no-dying.

May Buddhas and Bodhisattvas be our companions

on the wonderful path of practice. (o)

May we end all afflictions

so that understanding can arise,

the obstacles of unwholesome acts be dissolved,

and the fruit of awakening be fully realized. (o)

Namo Amitabha Buddhaya. (3 times) (ooo)

18.THE DIVINE GATHA

Gods, nagas, asuras and yakshas

Come here, with all your heart listen to the Dharma.

Protect the Buddha-dharma so that it may endure

And all may act in the spirit of the Buddha's teaching.

When you have come to hear the Dharma,

Whether you are under the earth or in the sky,

Look at all beings with the eyes of love.

Day and night abide in the right practice.

May the world always be safe and secure,

Impregnated by the merit of wisdom and love.

May all the obstacles of wrong doing be dissolved.

May we live behind afflictions

and know always how to touch peace and joy.

May the Sangha with determination observe the precepts,

Be diligent in the practice of meditative concentration.

May the flower of awakened understanding bloom beautifully

And everywhere may all species have happiness.

Namo the Dharma Protective
Bodhisattva Mahasattva. (3 times) (ooo)

BẢO ANH LẠC BOOKSHELF

Dr. Bhikṣuṇī TN Giới Hương composed

A. THE VIETNAMESE BOOKS

1. *Bồ-tát và Tánh Không Trong Kinh Tạng Pali và Đại Thừa* (Boddhisattva and Sunyata in the Early and Developed Buddhist Traditions).
2. *Ban Mai Xứ Ấn* (The Dawn in India), (3 tập).
3. *Vườn Nai – Chiếc Nôi* (Phật Giáo Deer Park–The Cradle of Buddhism).
4. *Quy Y Tam Bảo và Năm Giới* (Take Refuge in Three Gems and Keep the Five Precepts).
5. *Vòng Luân Hồi* (The Cycle of Life).
6. *Hoa Tuyết Milwaukee* (Snowflake in Milwaukee).
7. *Luân Hồi trong Lăng Kính Lăng Nghiêm* (The Rebirth in *Śūrangama* Sūtra).
8. *Nghi Thức Hộ Niệm, Cầu Siêu* (The Ritual for the Deceased).
9. *Quan Âm Quảng Trần* (The Commentary of Avalokiteśvara Bodhisattva).
10. *Nữ Tu và Tù Nhân Hoa Kỳ* (A Nun and American Inmates).
11. *Nếp Sống Tỉnh Thức của Đức Đạt Lai Lạt Ma Thứ XIV* (The Awakened Mind of the 14th Dalai Lama).
12. *A-Hàm: Mưa pháp chuyển hóa phiền não* (*Agama – A Dharma Rain transforms the Defilement*), 2 tập.
13. *Góp Từng Hạt Nắng Perris* (Collection of Sunlight in

Perris).

14. *Pháp Ngữ của Kinh Kim Cang* (The Key Words of Vajracchedikā-Prajñāpāramitā-Sūtra).
15. *Tập Thơ Nhạc Nắng Lăng Nghiêm* (Songs and Poems of Śūraṅgama Sunlight).
16. *Nét Bút Bên Song Cửa* (Reflections at the Temple Window).
17. *Máy Nghe MP3 Hương Sen* (Hương Sen Digital Mp3 Radio Speaker): Các Bài Giảng, Sách, Bài viết và Thơ Nhạc của Thích Nữ Giới Hương (383/201 bài).
18. *DVD Giới Thiệu về Chùa Hương Sen*, USA (Introduction on Huong Sen Temple).
19. *Ni Giới Việt Nam Hoằng Pháp tại Hoa Kỳ* (Sharing the Dharma - Vietnamese Buddhist Nuns in the United States).
20. *Tuyển Tập 40 Năm Tu Học & Hoằng Pháp của Ni sư Giới Hương* (Forty Years in the Dharma: A Life of Study and Service—Venerable Bhikkhuni Giới Hương), Thích Nữ Viên Quang, TN Viên Nhuận, TN Viên Tiến, and TN Viên Khuông.
21. *Tập Thơ Nhạc Lối Về Sen Nở* (*Songs and Poems of Lotus Blooming on the Way).*
22. *Nghi Thức Công Phu Khuya – Thần Chú Thủ Lăng Nghiêm* (Śūraṅgama Mantra).
23. *Nghi Thức Cầu An – Kinh Phổ Môn* (The Universal Door Sūtra).
24. *Nghi Thức Cầu An – Kinh Dược Sư* (The Medicine Buddha Sūtra).

25. *Nghi Thức Sám Hối Hồng Danh* (The Sūtra of Confession at many Buddha Titles).
26. *Nghi Thức Công Phu Chiều – Mông Sơn Thí Thực* (The Ritual Donating Food to Hungry Ghosts).
27. *Khóa Tịnh Độ – Kinh A Di Đà* (The Amitabha Buddha Sūtra).
28. *Nghi Thức Cúng Linh và Cầu Siêu* (The Rite for Deceased and Funeral Home).
29. *Nghi Lễ Hàng Ngày - 50 Kinh Tụng và các Lễ Vía trong Năm* (The Daily Chanting Rituals and Annual Ceremonies).
30. *Hương Đạo Trong Đời 2022* (Tuyển tập 60 Bài Thi trong Cuộc Thi Viết Văn Ứng Dụng Phật Pháp 2022 - A Collection of Writings on the Practicing of Buddhism in Daily Life in the Writing Contest 2022).
31. *Hương Pháp 2022* (Tuyển Tập Các Bài Thi Trúng Giải Cuộc Thi Viết Văn Ứng Dụng Phật Pháp 2022 - A Collection of the Winning Writings on the Practicing of Buddhism in Daily Life in the Writing Contest 2022).
32. *Giới Hương - Thơm Ngược Gió Ngàn*, Nguyên Hà.
33. *Pháp Ngữ Kinh Hoa Nghiêm* (2 tập). Thích Nữ Giới Hương.
34. *Tinh Hoa Kinh Hoa Nghiêm*. Thích Nữ Giới Hương. NXB Hương Sen.
35. *Phật Giáo và Đại Dịch Coronavirus Covid-19*. Thích Nữ Giới Hương.
36. *Phật Giáo – Tầm Nhìn Lịch Sử Và Thực Hành.* Hiệu đính: Thích Hạnh Chánh và Thích Nữ Giới Hương.

B. THE ENGLISH BOOKS

1. Boddhisattva and Sunyata in the Early and Developed Buddhist Traditions.
2. *Rebirth Views in the Śūraṅgama Sūtra.*
3. *Commentary of Avalokiteśvara Bodhisattva.*
4. *The Key Words in Vajracchedikā Sūtra.*
5. *Sārnātha-The Cradle of Buddhism in the Archeological View.*
6. *Take Refuge in the Three Gems and Keep the Five Precepts.*
7. *Cycle of Life.*
8. *Forty Years in the Dharma: A Life of Study and Service—Venerable Bhikkhuni Giới Hương.*
9. *Sharing the Dharma -Vietnamese Buddhist Nuns in the United States.*
10. *A Vietnamese Buddhist Nun and American Inmates.*
11. *Daily Monastic Chanting.*
12. *Weekly Buddhist Discourse Chanting.*
13. *Practice Meditation and Pure Land.*
14. *The Ceremony for Peace.*
15. *The Lunch Offering Ritual.*
16. *The Ritual Offering Food to Hungry Ghosts.*
17. *The Pureland Course of Amitabha Sutra.*
18. *The Medicine Buddha Sutra.*
19. *The New Year Ceremony.*
20. *The Great Parinirvana Ceremony.*

21. *The Buddha's Birthday Ceremony.*
22. *The Ullambana Festival (Parents' Day).*
23. *The Marriage Ceremony.*
24. *The Blessing Ceremony for The Deceased.*
25. *The Ceremony Praising Ancestral Masters.*
26. *The Enlightened Buddha Ceremony.*
27. *The Uposatha Ceremony (Reciting Precepts).*
28. *Buddhism: A Historical and Practical Vision.* Edited by Ven. Dr. Thich Hanh Chanh and Ven. Dr. Bhikṣuṇī TN Gioi Huong.
29. *Contribution of Buddhism For World Peace & Social Harmony.* Edited by Ven. Dr. Buddha Priya Mahathero and Ven. Dr. Bhikṣuṇī TN Gioi Huong.
30. *Global Spread of Buddhism with Special Reference to Sri Lanka.* Buddhist Studies Seminar in Kandy University. Edited by Dr. Ven. Kahawatte Siri Sumedha Thero and Dr. Bhikṣuṇī TN Gioi Huong.
31. *Buddhism In Sri Lanka During The Period of 19th to 21st Centuries.* Buddhist Studies Seminar in Colombo. Edited by Prof. Ven. Medagama Nandawansa and Dr. Bhikṣuṇī TN Gioi Huong.

C. THE BILINGUAL BOOKS (VIETNAMESE-ENGLISH)

1. *Bản Tin Hương Sen: Xuân, Phật Đản, Vu Lan (*Hương Sen Newsletter: Spring, Buddha Birthday and Vu Lan, annual/ Mỗi Năm).
2. *Danh Ngôn Nuôi Dưỡng Nhân Cách - Good Sentences*

Nurture a Good Manner.

3. *Văn Hóa Đặc Sắc của Nước Nhật Bản-Exploring the Unique Culture of Japan.*
4. *Sống An Lạc dù Đời không Đẹp như Mơ - Live Peacefully though Life is not Beautiful as a Dream.*
5. *Hãy Nói Lời Yêu Thương-Words of Love and Understanding.*
6. *Văn Hóa Cổ Kim qua Hành Hương Chiêm Bái -The Ancient- Present Culture in Pilgrim.*
7. *Nghệ Thuật Biết Sống - Art of Living.*

D. THE TRANSLATED BOOKS

1. *Xá Lợi Của Đức Phật* (Relics of the Buddha), Tham Weng Yew.
2. *Sen Nở Nơi Chốn Tử Tù* (Lotus in Prison), many authors.
3. *Chùa Việt Nam Hải Ngoại* (Overseas Vietnamese Buddhist Temples).
4. *Việt Nam Danh Lam Cổ Tự* (The Famous Ancient Buddhist Temples in Vietnam).
5. *Hương Sen, Thơ và Nhạc* – (Lotus Fragrance, Poem and Music).
6. *Phật Giáo-Một Bậc Đạo Sư, Nhiều Truyền Thống* (Buddhism: One Teacher – Many Traditions), Đức Đạt Lai Lạt Ma 14th & Ni Sư Thubten Chodren.
7. *Cách Chuẩn Bị Chết và Giúp Người Sắp Chết-Quan Điểm Phật Giáo* (Preparing for Death and Helping the Dying – A Buddhist Perspective).

BUDDHIST MUSIC ALBUMS

from POEMS of THÍCH NỮ GIỚI HƯƠNG

1. *Đào Xuân Lộng Ý Kinh* (The Buddha's Teachings Reflected in Cherry Flowers).
2. *Niềm Tin Tam Bảo* (Trust in the Three Gems).
3. *Trăng Tròn Nghìn Năm Đón Chờ Ai* (Who Is the Full Moon Waiting for for Over a Thousand Years?).
4. *Ánh Trăng Phật Pháp (*Moonlight of Dharma-Buddha).
5. *Bình Minh Tỉnh Thức* (Awakened Mind at the Dawn) (*Piano Variations for Meditation*).
6. *Tiếng Hát Già Lam* (Song from Temple).
7. *Cảnh Đẹp Chùa Xưa* (The Magnificent, Ancient Buddhist Temple).
8. Karaoke *Hoa Ưu Đàm Đã Nở* (An Udumbara Flower Is Blooming).
9. *Hương Sen Ca* (Hương Sen's Songs).
10. *Về Chùa Vui Tu* (Happily Go to Temple for Spiritual Practices).
11. *Gọi Nắng Xuân Về* (Call the Spring Sunlight).
12. *Đệ Tử Phật* (The Buddha's Disciples).

Please consult the ***Bảo Anh Lạc Bookshelf*** *at this website:*

http://huongsentemple.com/index.php/en/about-us/b-o-anh-l-c-bookshelf

THE RITUAL OFFERING FOOD TO HUNGRY GHOSTS

Author: Bao Anh Lac Bookshelf 61 - Huong Sen Buddhist Temple

HONG DUC PUBLISHING

Tel.: 024.39260024 - Fax : 024.39260031

Email: nhanxuatbanhongduc65@gmail.com

Responsible for publishing

Manager: **Bui Viet Bac**

Responsible for the content

Editor in Chief: **Ly Ba Toan**

Editor: **Phan Thi Ngoc Minh**

Presenter: **Vu Dinh Trong**

Editing the copy: **Vu Dinh Trong**

Printing quantity: 1,000 copies, Size: 14.5 x 20.5 cm

Printed at: Tram Anh Printing,

159/57 Bach Dang, Ward 2, Tan Binh District, HCM City.

Registration number: 3304-2023/CXBIPH/31-92/HĐ

ISBN: 978-604-108-209-3

Publishing decision: 325/QD-NXBHD dated September 29, 2023

Finished printing and deposit in the third quarter of 2023

www.ingramcontent.com/pod-product-compliance
Lightning Source LLC
LaVergne TN
LVHW022316200926
848481LV00004B/1363
* 9 7 9 8 3 4 9 5 3 0 2 1 0 *